TEACH
YOUR CHILD
TO FISH

FIVE MONEY HABITS EVERY CHILD
SHOULD MASTER

HOLLY D. REID, CPA

Teach Your Child to Fish
First Edition, March 2016

The Master Playbook
Atlanta, Georgia

Author: Holly D. Reid

Editor: Shayla Eaton, www.curiousediting.com

Cover: HappySelfPublishing.com

Print Edition ISBN-13: 978-0692703908
               ISBN-10: 069270390X

∽

*To my mother and father who supplied
unconditional love, wise counsel,
and a solid foundation.*

∽

DOWNLOAD THE PRINTABLE
TEACH YOUR CHILD TO FISH
WORKBOOK FREE!

Just to say thank you, I'd like to give you this supplemental workbook for FREE. This added bonus is packed with over twenty fun and easy-to-implement activities for parents to complete with their school-age children, kindergarten through high school.

Get the most out of this book by using the workbook as you tackle each money-management habit.

Download the printable workbook as my gift to you at www.TheMasterPlaybook.com

TABLE OF CONTENTS

Introduction..9

Chapter 1: Work Hard and Be Rewarded........15

Chapter 2: Spend Wisely and Consciously......37

Chapter 3: Save First and Consistently............57

Chapter 4: Use Credit Responsibly..................79

Chapter 5: Give Generously 99

Acknowledgements.......................................117

About the Author...119

Connect with the Author 121

INTRODUCTION

"Give a man a fish and he will eat for a day.
Teach a man to fish and he'll eat for a lifetime."

—Chinese Proverb

I have a special memory of my dad taking me and my three sisters on our first fishing trip. As I reflect, I can imagine my dad being a little excited as he planned to teach and expose his daughters to one of his favorite pastimes. The car was loaded with everything we'd need to make this fishing trip a success: live bait, fishing rods, snacks, and huge baseball caps to shield our young faces from the sun.

Once we arrived and settled onto the bank, I'm sure my dad immediately regretted ever bringing us.

We didn't want to hook the worms. We didn't like the flies. We didn't want to be outside. We didn't want to sit and wait. And the greatest disappointment of all, we didn't catch any fish. It was an epic fail, with the exception that he *required* us to try and *encouraged* us to give fishing a chance, even if only for a little while.

My sisters and I by no means mastered the art of fishing that day. But looking back, I'm grateful my dad taught us how to fish.

And now, you're going to teach your child how to fish.

Teach Your Child to Fish provides guiding principles and practical activities to teach the next generation money-management concepts and a critical life skill they should adopt as they begin to understand money. The guiding principles are supported by scripture to highlight and reinforce the wisdom found within the Bible. No matter the version you chose, the Bible is full of practical instruction and wise counsel that children can comprehend. The recommended activities included in each chapter are designed to enforce a key money-management concept and are easy and fun to implement. As an added benefit, I've created a supplemental workbook you can download that provides templates and specific instructions for select activities.

Take all the successes and failures you've had with money management and think of the lessons you've learned along the way. What would you teach your younger self about money if you had the opportunity? Would you tell yourself to save more? Would you make different choices to avoid debt? Most adults wish they had received more exposure to financial literacy and money management earlier in life, and more importantly, before they were out on their own.

The absence of financial literacy at home *and* in our schools creates a society filled with victims of the consumer culture, bound in debt, and working beyond retirement age—not because they want to, but because they have to. Today's youth face a future of similar obstacles because they are learning sound financial concepts and practicing ideal money-management habits too late in life.

As a Certified Public Accountant and finance professional, I have taught financial literacy to students of all ages and have coached young adults toward achieving their financial goals. While I am not yet a parent, I can clearly see the need and understand that *together*, we can provide the building blocks for future generations to be successful with money. My interaction with young people, hearing their skewed money beliefs firsthand, only confirms the need for parents (and the village) to offer more insight and dialogue when it comes to money management.

Proverbs 22:6 (NIV) calls us to give proper instruction to a child: "Train up a child in the way he should go, and even when he is old he will not depart from it." And the truth is, parents are far better suited than anyone else to teach financial education, because whether you realize it or not, your child is already learning from you through observation. If they are not learning from you, they are learning from other influential adults, whether that person happens to be family, a friend, or a stranger they see in the media. Use this time to *intentionally* help them establish healthy money habits and maneuver through the potential pitfalls money management may bring.

Most parents want the very best for their child and will make the time to talk about the birds and the bees, the dangers of drug use, and the benefits of a pursuing higher education. By following my lead, you can begin to build and create a legacy of healthy financial habits for generations to come by sharing the financial principles and implementing the activities found in this helpful lesson book. By establishing an open dialogue about money, and modeling and practicing healthy money habits with your children, you will provide the building blocks for a healthy financial future.

As parents, you will be able to guide your children through the fundamentals of money management (knowledge) and bring the concepts to life through everyday activities (application). This book doesn't just give you the tools—it tells you how to implement them. No one is born knowing how to fish. They must be taught and instructed. Similarly, once your child is taught the rules and given the tools for money management, they can be used for a lifetime.

I guarantee the lessons shared and practiced in this book will serve as a foundation that results in a more financially stable and secure legacy for generations to come. The money habits and recommendations presented establish a foundation for building wealth and developing a child's financial intelligence.

Don't you wish someone would've taken the time to teach you money-management concepts at a young age? Think for a moment what your life would be like. Now think about what this means for your children. You can break the chains of poor money habits so that your child will never face mounds of consumer debt or the dreaded paycheck-to-paycheck living. You could change your child's life.

Take advantage of this resource today and share the money-management habits your children will *need* and will rely on to establish their own financial legacy. Go ahead, teach your child to fish, and give them the skills they will use for a lifetime.

CHAPTER 1

WORK HARD AND
BE REWARDED

"Good planning and hard work lead to prosperity,
but hasty shortcuts lead to poverty."

—Proverbs 21:5 (NLT)

As a child, I had a habit of waiting until the last minute to ask my dad for money for a field trip scheduled for the next day. I could sense a hint of frustration as he pulled out his wallet or went to his tall dresser to pull a few dollars together so I could enjoy a Happy Meal® or an ice cream cone on the field trip. I never really understood the source of his frustration, since my dad always had the money. I would see our lunch money stacked on his dresser every day of the week, so I thought, "Money came from my dad."

As a child, I had no idea five dollars was so hard to come by at nine o'clock at night, right before bedtime, or six o'clock in the morning right before I was to catch the school bus. Oblivious to the intentional budgeting and planning my dad did to provide for us, I asked for the money I needed or wanted and was rarely told no.

When raising money-smart adults, one of the first concepts they must grasp is that money comes from hard work and not from their parents, grandparents, and certainly not from trees.

I didn't grasp that concept as a child. But your children *can*.

This chapter dives into three main topics: why we work, the benefits of hard work, and discovering work.

End-of-chapter activities enforce the concept of working hard as well as practical ways to earn money as a child or teenager. Each activity promotes the values of responsibility, integrity, and teamwork.

Why We Work

To lay the foundation, let's begin with why we work. In the beginning, God created the heaven and the earth. In Genesis, God set the example for us to work when He created and filled the universe in six days. Later, He bans Adam and Eve (mankind) from working in the Garden of Eden, once they ate from the Tree of Knowledge.

*"So the Lord God banished him from the Garden of Eden **to work** the ground from which he had been taken."*

—Genesis 3:23 (NIV)

This is followed in Exodus 20:9 (NLV) when God gives the universal command on work:

"You have six days each week for your ordinary work."

Said more plainly, we have been given a responsibility by God to work and to take care of the earth and the things in it. These are excellent scriptures to read and reference to your children to introduce the concept of work and begin a discussion about why we work.

In being obedient to God's command to work, we are called to give God our best in whatever we do. Let's pause there, because this is where you, as a parent, have to park any ill feelings or negative remarks you may have about your current job or profession. Instead, we need to teach our children to be obedient and diligent with the task or job they are assigned to complete, by giving our best, whether they like it or not. In fact, Scripture warns us about not giving our best or being lazy when we should be working. Proverbs 6:6–11 (NLT) instructs us to be like the ant:

> *"Take a lesson from the ants, you lazybones.*
> *Learn from their ways and become wise!*
> *Though they have no prince*
> *or governor or ruler to make them work,*
> *they labor hard all summer,*
> *gathering food for the winter."*

Here's the warning starting in verse 9:

> *"But you, lazybones, how long will you sleep?*
> *When will you wake up?*

A little extra sleep, a little more slumber,
a little folding of the hands to rest—
then poverty will pounce on you like a bandit;
scarcity will attack you like an armed robber.

Children love story time, but learning about hard work may lull them to sleep faster than the storybook. Make the topic of hard work and rewards interesting by telling them the story of the ant. In this passage, the ant, though small, can be observed being very busy and productive throughout the day. The ant is gathering grains of food and supplies to build its home. Using this example, the lesson to our children is to be diligent and productive when they work, or reap the consequences of no reward.

The Benefits of Hard Work and Its Reward

Work requires our full effort, and the ability to work is a blessing and something we should teach our children to be thankful for. To keep it simple, there are two primary benefits of hard work:

1. **To meet our needs.** This means we are able to earn money to support the things that are essential in life like living in a safe place,

buying foods to help us grow and become stronger, and buying clothes. As a bonus, hard work allows us to buy items we want for our children like video games, bikes, dolls, or accessories.

2. **To make a profit and build wealth.** Once our basic needs are met, we are stewards over the remaining funds to be spent responsibly. In the upcoming chapters, we will discuss how this money should be spent wisely, saved, invested, and shared with others.

Beyond money to meet our needs and to build wealth, working hard also feeds and satisfies the soul, creates happiness, and provides an outlet to develop and practice leadership skills. From the perspective of our children, here's a quick list of examples you can share where the reward for hard work is not tied to money:

a. **Learning new things and becoming smarter:** Exercising the mind yields tangible results. For example, memorizing speeches for a class or performance can help children learn new words and increase their vocabulary. Completing homework allows children to practice reading or writing to become a better student.

b. Increasing confidence and self-worth: Sharing natural gifts and talents with others can increase self-esteem, especially when compared to someone who may find the same task or job more difficult. Think of a skill that comes naturally to your child. Maybe they have an outgoing personality and aren't afraid to speak or perform for a crowd; or maybe they have a technical aptitude and can operate various devices with little instruction or guidance. They have skills that may come very easy to them, but can prove very difficult to another.

c. Making a difference: Giving and being helpful to others can be philanthropic. Through donations of their gently used items or volunteering to help with a service to the community like delivering food, children will gain a sense of empathy for those who are unable to work due to illness, tragedy, or disaster. They can see immediately how their contribution can help someone or make a difference in their community.

Being rewarded for hard work can come in many forms, whether it's through money, gifts, trophies, or recognition. In what way does your child like to be rewarded? You can begin to focus on and practice rewarding your child for the work they do, whether it's in and around the house, serving in church, or a job well done in school.

As a parent, if you are able to reward your children with money, I recommend paying a commission versus an allowance. An allowance simply pays your child a set amount each day or each week with very little accountability or ownership. It has the potential to promote a sense of entitlement or a level of expectancy that you do not have to work to get paid. In contrast, a commission will encourage ownership and accountability as well as connect hard work to rewards when these elements exist:

- **Pay your child for some chores.** The rationale is there are some chores your child should do because they are deemed family responsibilities. As the parent, you can assign four to six chores that fall into the pay category with the understanding that the goal is to associate hard work with earning the reward of money.

- **Track each chore as "Complete" on a daily basis.** If the chore was not completed on that day, your child should not get paid. This presents the opportunity to teach honesty and ownership while encouraging repetition and consistency of daily tasks.

- **Reward your child immediately.** Pay the earned commissions daily or weekly. This builds an immediate connection between the chores they did and the reward they received.

As an example, assign five commissionable chores worth $0.05 to $0.20 each. This gives your child the potential to earn $0.25 to $1 each day. The lessons, however, should not stop here. Follow the money and add requirements for how it should be spent. Consider adding a rule that requires a portion of what they earn be saved, invested, and donated. We'll address all of these options in later chapters.

Discovering Work

While work is required and expected, it's important for parents to help their children discover a career that fits their personality, interests, and purpose in life, as designed by God. (See Psalm 90:17, NIV)

We are all uniquely made with different skills and talents we can offer and contribute to society.

We've all heard the cliché: "Do something you enjoy and you'll never work a day in your life." As parents, I encourage you to begin to subscribe to this mantra and actively cultivate your child's natural gifts, talents, and interests at a young age. You want to instill a deeper, long-lasting desire to help your child find and fulfill their purpose that also helps them meet their everyday needs and wants.

Practice paying attention to the activities and subject matter your children show interest in or the activities they express joy in doing, and help nurture and support those interests. The Montessori Method of education has taken the lead using this same practice where the emphasis is placed on a child's natural psychological, physical, and social development. Montessori education allows students to be active participants in deciding what their focus of learning will be, working within parameters set by their teachers.[1] As parents, you can take the same approach.

---

1 For more on Montessori, read: http://amshq.org/Montessori-Education/Introduction-to-Montessori/Benefits-of-Montessori

I believe we are born and designed to fulfill a purpose in this world. Everyone has a talent or gift that they should seek to identify, cultivate, and use to contribute to society. So whether your child is eight or eighteen, there's never a wrong time to help them explore their interests.

As with everything else in life, kids learn best by example. If you enjoy your work or have a successful career, use this time to share with your children what you do for a living and why you enjoy your work. Is it the people you meet and help along the way? Is it the excitement of visiting different places and learning something new? Jump in and share your personal "discovering work" experiences with your children so they can better understand and appreciate how hard you work for them!

Feed Their Entrepreneurial Spirit

As you learn and observe, and as your child expresses interest in certain subjects or activities, be sure to encourage and feed your child's entrepreneurial spirit. The building blocks for a young entrepreneur first begin with one idea.

As evident by the creation of Facebook or the successful online Groupon business, there are a host of young people—a new generation of entrepreneurs—starting businesses and nonprofit organizations based on their interests. Their creativity and passion shine through as they make consumer products like facial scrubs and bracelets; or begin a socially conscious movement like launching a recycling program or organizing book drives to encourage literacy in underserved communities. A few recent examples that have received national attention include:

- Moziah Bridges, founder of Mo's Bows, who learned how to sew his own bowties with the help of his grandmother. The eleven-year-old began selling his creations on Etsy, and his products were soon picked up by boutiques in several southern states.[2]

- Madison Robinson, founder of Fish Flops at age fifteen. She first had the idea for light-up flip flops for kids when she was only eight years old. Seven years later, Robinson Fish

---

2   Charlotte Lytton. "Teen Entrepreneurs Making Millions." http://www.cnn.com/2014/12/08/business/teen-entrepreneurs-making-millions/

Flops are being sold in national department stores like Nordstrom.[3]

- Aireal Taylor, founder of KidzCab, a Michigan-based transportation service for children ages four to sixteen.[4] She discovered her business idea while completing a marketing assignment in college. The service drives children to and from school and for extracurricular activities.

There are thousands of other success stories that never receive national attention. Take my sister, Toni, for example. She is the ultimate entrepreneur. Since I can remember, she paved her own way to earn money. She established an impeccable work ethic early on, largely attributed to the examples set by my parents, and would branch out to pursue the things she wanted in life. In high school, she outperformed public school vending machines by offering greater inventory variety and lower prices.

---

3 Ibid.

4 http://www.blackenterprise.com/career/young-entrepreneur-turns-class-project-into-successful-kids-transportation-company/.

In college, she earned extra money making hand-sized Rice Krispy treats and sold them as late-night snacks to students on campus. Even today, she works for herself and loves her independence and flexibility. It is through her entrepreneurial trials and successes as a teenager and young adult, in addition to my parents' encouragement, that she developed the wisdom and confidence that she can do anything she sets her mind to accomplish.

Perhaps your youngster already has an idea that you didn't pay much attention to before reading this book. Now is the time to encourage their creativity and imagination and nurture their ideas. The earlier we teach our children to take risks, the sooner they learn to fail. The more they fail, the more they learn and are able to develop better ideas that lead to success. When a fish slips the hook and gets away, it's easy to get frustrated and give up, but every fishing failure can teach you something about your gear or your technique. Within entrepreneurship, you have to pay attention to the lessons because they can make you better. In the recommended activities section, I will share a few ideas to help you cultivate the entrepreneurial spirit within your child. For more, listen to a TedTalk, *Let's Raise Kids to Be Entrepreneurs*, delivered by

Cameron Herold, the entrepreneur best known for his company 1-800-GOT-JUNK?.[5]

Recommended Activities:

Here are a few recommended activities you can use to teach your children about hard work and its rewards.

🐟 **Household chores.** As we teach children about hard work, the starting point should be in the home. Whether you have a toddler or a teenager, it's easy to find chores around the house to teach children about hard work. This is most commonly everyone's first experience in learning a good work ethic.

Being raised with three older sisters, there was plenty to be done and I'm certain we worked every variation of the chore list, including assigning specific chores by person, rotating chores by day of the week, and a combination of the two meth-

---

5   Watch the TedTalk at: https://www.ted.com/talks/cameron_herold_let_s_raise_kids_to_be_entrepreneurs?language=en

ods. Whatever method you chose, just make sure your child is introduced to having chores as they grow up. This can begin as early as three years old and evolve as they get older. Start with simple tasks that can be completed consistently. The tasks will begin to instill a level of responsibility like picking up toys, cleaning their room, walking the dog, preparing lunch for the family, etc. And then reward them immediately with things they value like watching TV, playing video games, having dessert, or earning money. The goal is to associate hard work with *rewards*. No matter the predetermined reward, I would encourage you to make it interactive and visually track the task with the payment to encourage accountability.

Warning: Try to avoid paying your children to be good students. The reward there is getting great grades and graduating to the next level.

Encourage passion and innovation. I believe our truest passions emerge in childhood. Take note of the things your child gravitates toward. What do they absolutely love to do? Play outside? Help others? Perform magic tricks? Conduct scientific experiments? This will not only serve them well when determining their life work, but it will also be a great starting point as you begin to teach them about giving, which we will discuss in Chapter 5.

Once they have established what they like to do, have them brainstorm and create a way to make money. This will encourage creativity, which births innovation. Does your child enjoy writing? Consider starting a blog. Is your daughter tech-savvy and creative? Maybe she would be interested in designing websites. Does your son make an instant connection with the neighbor's dog? Perhaps he could start a dog-walking business.[6] Children are so talented—it is absolutely amazing the unlimited number of ways they can begin to earn money.

🐟 **Volunteer for a cause.** Find a cause or charity that you or your child feels passionate about and make it a point to volunteer your time as a family. Consider a food or clothing bank, planting trees, delivering food to the disabled or elderly. Discuss what task or activity they enjoyed the most/least. And why? How did their work today help someone else?

---

6 For more ideas, read: http://kidmoney.about.com/od/jobsforkids/fl/Unique-Business-Ideas-for-Kids.htm.

Name that job. In your everyday errands and routine, ask your child to name or identify at least three jobs being performed. For example, during a visit to a grocery store, your child may notice the person stocking the shelves, the butcher at the meat counter chopping meat, and the cashier adding the items being purchased. Ask your child why the job is important and how they are helping people. This exercise can be done in almost any environment to raise awareness that all work is important.

This was an idea my dad implemented with my nephew, Michael, as he flew between Texas and Georgia a few times a year to visit family. My dad prompted Michael to notice and call out the work of the pilot, the airplane crew, baggage handlers, and the airline stewardess. It heightened his awareness of his surroundings and created a platform for Michael to ask questions about things he saw or didn't understand.

Other ways to introduce and teach your children about hard work is to actively participate in established initiatives like Take Your Child to Work Day and Career Day in their classroom or through organizations like Girl Scouts of America. As they get older, they can participate in job shadowing, apprenticeships, and internship programs.

Final Thoughts

In this chapter, we addressed hard work and practical ways to help children identify the many ways people contribute to society. Helping your child understand why we work is the foundation to raising responsible and financially conscious adults. Understanding the benefits of hard work will allow your child to see how working not only helps them meet monetary needs, but also supports their personal development and strengthens their communities.

Finally, helping your child discover the work that may be best for them will give them a head start to focus on the things they enjoy doing and how they can make money from it using innovation, creativity, and their natural gifts and talents. As an added bonus, the more encouragement received in this area, the more our children will learn to take risks and fail *toward* success.

In the next chapter, we will discuss how to develop smart spending habits with your children. The more guidance and exposure they receive to money management, the greater their financial future will be.

Get the most out of this book by using the supplemental workbook as you tackle each money-management habit.

To reinforce the lessons you've learned in Chapter 1: Work Hard & Be Rewarded, Refer to pages 5 – 10 in the workbook.

Download the printable workbook at
www.TheMasterPlaybook.com/free-workbook

CHAPTER 2

SPEND WISELY AND CONSCIOUSLY

"The wise have wealth and luxury,
but fools spend whatever they get."

—Proverbs 21:20 (NLT)

W hat shapes children's spending habits? Often, parents or influential people in their lives. Spending habits can also be shaped by society and cultural trends, peer pressure, the media, and religious or spiritual beliefs. They are developed over time through observation and practice. As parents, you must equip your child with knowledge, help them understand their choices, and allow them to make decisions as they mature.

The objective of this chapter is to help your child develop healthy spending habits. It is not common sense – instead it is a *learned behavior*. Spending wisely and consciously means you will help guide your child to think and then spend their money in the smartest and most productive way possible.

> *"We buy things we don't need with money we don't have to impress people we don't like."*
>
> —Dave Ramsey

Let's first take a look at our environment. Today's corporations spend millions of dollars each year targeting parents and kids to become their next loyal consumer. Marketers make it their job to tell us what we need and what we should desire to attain. These experts have mastered the art of influence and temptation so well that even as conscious adults, we fall prey to their marketing tactics. Imagine how easy it is for your child to be tempted.

Have you ever walked into Walmart, Target, or the Dollar Tree to purchase one or two items and came out instead with a shopping cart full of things not on your list? At one time or another, we've all been guilty of it. Retail giants and grocery stores line their checkout lanes with items like gum, candy bars, and small toys that encourage impulse purchases—often priced at a premium, when compared to the same item sold in a bundle in the candy aisle. Beyond the stores, marketing messages are everywhere! Television commercials, custom pop-up ads tailored to sites you've visited or searches you've previously conducted, electronic billboards, and now even in most movie theaters, we are bombarded with advertisements.

Now, narrow your focus to the world of advertising from your *child's* point of view. Consider the peer pressure a child must experience when half the class is sporting the latest gadget or fashion trend. Even during my school days, kids formed social clubs where they all wore the same name-brand clothing or they set dates to all go purchase the latest athletic shoe, watch, or concert tickets together. Now, it's not just the shoes you wear, but the latest phone, tablet, and video games that you *have* to buy if you want to be the cool kid at the table. My household certainly didn't have the disposable income for the luxuries I just described. In retrospect, it sounds ridiculous, but in the perspective of a child, it could potentially place them in a position as being a social outcast. I highlight these examples to raise awareness around the social pressure a child may experience and how potentially damaging it can be the earlier these messages are not combatted with values and healthy habits.

As they get a little older, outside influences like marketing tactics and peer pressure make developing healthy spending habits an even more critical skill to practice and master. When you fish around others, sometimes your lines get crossed. This concept certainly applies when it comes to peer pressure. As parents, you have the power to expose and override marketing tactics by teaching your children to be conscious consumers. It begins by providing your child with knowledge and information. Then, empower them to think and ask key questions to develop their financial intelligence.

The goal is to build the muscle memory for your child to instinctively ask themselves key questions before making a purchase. Let's examine the four questions they can ponder before spending their hard-earned money:

Question 1: Is it a need or a want? Do I really need it? **Needs vs. Wants** — Giving your child the skills to distinguish between needs and wants may be the most important and the most challenging lesson you can teach your child. The traditional Needs categories will be covered by you: shelter, food, basic clothing, and utilities—so I've devised a list of items that could be categorized as Needs from a child's perspective:

- Educational tools, resources, or materials: items that enhance their intelligence, teaches them a useful skill, or helps with school projects or homework. For example, flash cards, a calculator, or books.

- Passion purchases: items that cultivate or promote an expressed interest, gift, or talent. For example, a musical instrument, art supplies, or cookware to help them develop their skills.

All other items that fall out of these categories are considered wants. And while it is okay to allow them to indulge and enjoy items purely for entertainment, the idea is to make it a thoughtful decision so over time they can clearly distinguish between needs and wants.

Question 2: Is it age or morally appropriate?

Deny Your Child—I hereby give you permission to tell your child no. Their world will not traumatically come to an end if they don't get the M-rated video game they keep asking for. When a child sees something and wants it immediately, it can be a struggle to tell them no, or to calm the emotional explosion that happens when this occurs; but it's all a part of the process. They must be denied and told that they can't have everything they want— even if other parents buy it for their kids. "You are not old enough" or "This does not promote our value system" are two simple phrases you can use to explain why they can't have a desired item.

Question 3: Is this something I can wait to have? Is it worth it, or should I continue to save? Is this a long-term or short-term purchase?

Delayed Gratification—The goal is to help your children avoid or curb impulse purchasing. When they see something they want, make them wait a day or more. Perhaps they need to save more of their own money before they can afford the item that they really want. We will touch on this subject in detail in Chapter 3.

As your son or daughter gets older, you also want them to practice thinking long-term and whether this is the best purchase for today. Consider whether the desired purchase, like a pair of Nike Air Jordans or the first edition drone, will be useful and beneficial over the next three months or if its usefulness will extend beyond twelve months. Questions you can ask include, Will this style be popular one year from now or will everyone be on to the next great thing? When the new model comes out in a few months, will I want that one too?

Question 4: Who will this help and why? Who could this potentially hurt if I make this purchase? **Impact to Me and My Community**—As your child gets older, starting around twelve years old, you should add this question to their purchasing decisions and connect spending money with also being a moral decision. After all, we are all stewards of the blessings given to us and will be held accountable for the way we use our resources.

"Yes, each of us will give a personal account to God."
—Romans 14:12 (NLT)

Encourage your child to research the company. Who is selling the product or service? Are they socially responsible to the community and the things we care about? What do reliable news sources say about the company or product? Do they want to support this company? Why? Why not?

The new generation is *obsessed* with social good companies. They care and are more in tune with what companies are doing in the community and around issues that are important to them. This question holds relevant and is a great segue when you begin to teach your children about investing, which I will address in detail in Chapter 3. The objective is to align their spending with their personal value system. Matthew 6:21 (NIV) says, "For where your treasure is, there your heart will be also."

Benefits of Teaching Good Spending Habits Early

Teaching young children good spending habits early can really pay off. It certainly paid off for me.

Shopping with my Mom was always a field trip. We would visit more than one store and most everything was bought on sale. Her shopping trips weren't necessarily planned events, but she had a magnetic draw to the sale and clearance racks (even to this day). I don't think I've ever seen her pay full price for anything. My mom is a whiz at stretching a dollar. It's evident from pictures of the four of us wearing matching, handmade dresses and my instant recall of wearing my sister's hand-me-downs year after year. It wasn't until my middle and high school years that I realized how practical yet creative my mom was with money. I was never the most fashionable kid on the block, but my mom's resourcefulness taught me to be frugal and to bargain-shop far sooner than most teenagers.

As you work your way to the recommended activities at the end of the chapter, your child will practice and explore healthy spending habits like setting financial goals, creating a budget, tracking their spending, and comparison shopping. As you promote and practice these healthy habits with your child, they will be equipped to more wisely tackle spending as adults. They will be able to set goals for themselves and use visualizations and affirmations that will greatly increase their chances to achieve them. They will be proactive, think ahead, and plan their spending and avoid or minimize impulse shopping. They will look for the best price and deals that will ultimately save them money. They will practice tracking their spending and creating budgets far sooner than their peers. They will learn to be intentional in their spending and tell their money where to go.

As a result of working through the activities, they will also learn through their mistakes. When they make a mistake, embrace their lessons in failure. Allow your child to make money mistakes so they can experience the consequences or discomfort of making poor money decisions. Use their money mistakes as teaching moments so they too will experience the satisfaction of saving patiently or waiting to purchase something they really want. With your guidance and the open dialogue created with your child, you can share your spending mistakes and the lessons you've learned along the way as well.

Recommended Activities:

Here are the recommended activities to promote healthy spending habits. Select one or all to begin teaching and practicing healthy spending habits with your children today:

- **Goal-setting with your children.** Statistics show that individuals are far more likely to achieve *written* goals as opposed to goals that are not written down. Even Scripture instructs us to write our vision (Habakkuk 2:2). How much more successful would your children be if they mastered goal-setting at a young age?

Have your child write a financial goal they would like to achieve in the next two to three weeks and place it on their bedroom wall, the refrigerator, or some other public space in the home where they will see it every day.

Example goal statements include: I will save $10 by January 31st. I will invest $3 for every $5 I earn this month. I will give $20 to [enter favorite charity, church, school] by December 1st.

Alternatively, if your child is more visual and creative by nature, consider creating a vision board together. Instead of writing their goals down in words, they can use images to depict their goals. They can create a digital vision board through offerings like Pic Stitch or Pinterest, or they can manually cut pictures from magazines or online images to create a physical vision board.

Help them dream and set their sights to create stretch goals for themselves later in life. This activity can be used for many other areas in your children's lives, so don't be afraid to help them set financial, academic, or extracurricular goals in their life as well. Maybe your child is learning to play the piano. Help them write a goal that says how many times they will practice without their instructor this week.

Once the goal has been achieved, be sure to acknowledge their accomplishment and have small celebrations. You may be surprised at how quickly your child masters this life skill.

Budgeting 101. A popular way to teach children about spending their money wisely is by teaching them a simple way to budget their spending using 3 categories: Save, Spend and Give. You can use mason jars or envelopes to distinguish the money into each category of spending. Have your child draw pictures of what he or she wants on each envelope or jar label. As they become more sophisticated and tech savvy, they can use electronic tools like budgeting apps to track their money.

Plan your spending. Shop with a list and stick to it. This is an easy exercise that your child can help participate in any day of the week. You can make a list for back-to-school shopping, grocery shopping where they specifically write the items they would like to eat for breakfast or lunch, a school project, or for a sport they are participating in. For teens, help them think through everything they may need for one week, make a list, and allow them to handle the responsibility for the week. Use pen and paper or one of the many electronic apps, like AnyList or Our-Groceries, to get a few routine tasks started and finished.

Comparison shop before you buy. Another great habit is to look for a great deal on the things needed. Check out sales and discount codes online for the store you plan to visit or specifically for the item you plan to purchase. If going to a grocery store or big retail store, have your child look up coupons for items on your list that they can either cut out, print out, or upload on an app for the store. I am a fan of the RedLaser app and I always check the Retail Me Not site before making a purchase online.

Distinguish between needs vs. wants. Here's a quick and practical exercise you can use to drive home your child's understanding of needs and wants and help them distinguish between the two: Take a blank sheet of paper or use a white board and create two columns. Label one column NEEDS and the second column WANTS. Call out different items in your home and ask your child to write them under the category. Once you've called out about ten items, go back and discuss why they think the item is categorized as a Need or Want.

🐟 **Ask for a student discount.** There are typically two stages in life when you get more discounts than normal: as a student and as a senior citizen. My opinion is that companies are trying to build a young customer base, and student discounts may attract them. Wireless is one of the most popular categories where big telecom companies like AT&T, Sprint, and Verizon offer 10 percent or more to students. Auto insurance companies offer teen drivers discounts up to 20 percent when they complete driver's education classes or earn good grades.

🐟 **Track your spending.** This is where budgeting begins! Practice creating small budgets and make them more advanced as your children get older. For younger children, start by creating a budget for a school project. Make a shopping list before you go to the store and include two columns. In Column 1, input an estimated amount you plan to spend next to each item listed. Make your purchases and return to this exercise. Once you return from the store, review your receipts and enter the amount you actually spent in Column 2. Calculate the difference. Were you over, under, or right on target with your estimates?

For older children (ages thirteen and older), have your child practice creating a budget for the school year. Create a budget one semester or quarter at a time. Now they can begin creating a budget using broader spending categories like school clothes/uniforms, school supplies, class-specific projects, social events like prom, birthday gifts, and parties.

Have a household budget in place and share it with your child. Let them see and observe you working on it and updating it month to month. Make it a priority, and your child will too.

This activity will begin to give your child insight into how much things cost and how the things they ask for can really add up. After completing these activities, they'll be able to think through what that they need so they aren't making multiple trips to the store. Another benefit is that you can begin to purchase things as they go on sale because you have mapped out the need in advance.

Make giving a part of your spending plan. Giving should come from the heart. Ask your child how they would like to help others. The goal is to make giving genuine and authentic and not something they are made or forced to do. Model giving with all of your resources. Begin by volunteering your time. Move to donating gently used possessions, like toys or clothing. Incorporate giving monetary gifts and donations whether it's to a homeless shelter or a charity where they can hand-deliver their gift.

Shopping spree. This activity will teach comparison shopping and the value of a dollar. Shop at a consignment store for like-new or gently used items at a fraction of the cost. Compare the prices you paid in the consignment store to the retail value of the same or similar item either online or from the mall. Explain how over time this can add up to serious money that they can use for other things, like saving, investing, or giving.

Join the mailing list and download the free supplemental workbook I've created to support select activities within this book.

Final Thoughts

You just learned practical strategies to spend wisely and consciously with your children. Whether they are just learning about money or managing money on a daily basis, these tips and activities (when practiced) will teach them to be responsible and money-conscious adults.

This is a time to model the behavior you are teaching your children. This is not a time for "Do as I say, not as I do." Allow your children to observe you taking part in these healthy spending habits, and they are likely to follow suit. The bonus of teaching your children these spending habits is that it will hold you accountable to improve in areas where you may be challenged.

In the next chapter, I will share the fundamentals of savings and how it can be encouraged and practiced at an early age. Read on to better understand the legacy you create by teaching your children to save first and to invest for the future.

Get the most out of this book by using the supplemental workbook as you tackle each money-management habit.

To reinforce the lessons you've learned in Chapter 2: Spend Wisely and Consciously, Refer to pages 11 – 16 in the workbook.

Download the printable workbook at
www.TheMasterPlaybook.com/free-workbook

CHAPTER 3

SAVE FIRST AND CONSISTENTLY

"But divide your investments among many places,
for you do not know what risks might lie ahead."

—Ecclesiastes 11:2 (NLT)

Growing up, I can remember being told to save, but I don't ever recall doing it in a meaningful way. With no allowance or commission from my parents, I didn't have a consistent flow of money during my school-age years. It wasn't until my college years that I began working a few hours a week, but most of it went to support my social life. Looking back, I also didn't have anything I considered critical to save for, primarily because my parents set the expectation early on for what we could and could not have—none of us had cars in high school because of the absorbent insurance costs to cover four girls under the age of twenty—or they simply saved and provided it for us. It was a blessing to have parents who could provide, but there were valuable, teachable moments related to saving money that my sisters and I were forced to learn later in life.

This chapter is all about identifying and creating those teachable moments and allowing children to practice them earlier in life to create a healthy money habit of saving *first* and saving consistently. We want to focus our efforts on saving for an item they are unable to purchase with a few dollars.

Research shows that Americans are not saving as they should. GOBankingRates conducted a survey of five thousand people and found nearly half didn't have any savings. Twenty-eight percent of those surveyed had nothing in their savings accounts and another 21 percent didn't even have a savings account. Sadly, for those with savings, the survey found just 29 percent of them had one thousand dollars or more.[7] These are the kind of statistics we should aim to improve.

When it comes to saving money, the instant gratification of spending the money now is far more attractive than saving for a rainy day. I'm not sure that feeling ever goes away for most people, so it remains critically important to teach our children to make saving money a priority and to make it fun! While they are young, there is an opportunity for them to master this life skill of delayed gratification and develop a savings habit that will help them build long-term, generational wealth.

Teach Your Child How to Save

In developing the saving habit, it's important to equip your kids with effective savings strategies. We are not going to focus on how much to save; rather the focus will be to save something—whatever portion you deem appropriate—and to do it first, not last.

---

7   Elyssa Kirkham. "62% of Americans Have Under $1,000 in Savings, Survey Finds." http://www.gobankingrates.com/savings-account/62-percent-americans-under-1000-savings-survey-finds/.

When children give their money a job, they will be far more likely to stay on the path to achieve what they want longer. Meaning, we should teach our children to assign every dollar they earn and receive to a specific purpose. This is where the goal-setting activity mentioned at the end of Chapter 2 will come in handy. You want to generate a level of excitement and determination for putting money aside to match the excitement they have when they are preparing to spend money.

We want to make saving intentional and purposeful so they are excited to reach their goal. Start by structuring their savings into two areas: short-term and long-term. Help your child visually understand that some items will take longer than others to save for. Using saving jars as our primary example, the short-term savings container might have a picture of a specific toy, while the long-term container might have a picture of a trip to Disneyland. This visualization exercise can continue to be used as children get older and when they want more expensive possessions like cars or an apartment.

For now, buy your child a fun piggy bank or decorate a money savings jar with them. For older kids, go with them to open a savings account.

Make it a celebration when they place their money in the bank. My first savings account was certainly eventful. At eighteen years old, I had just graduated from high school and had my sights on attending college in the Fall. I had received cash and several checks as graduation gifts, but didn't have anywhere to put the money. It was then that my mom took me to open a savings account at our neighborhood credit union. I was so excited and felt as though I was completing one of the rites of passage into adulthood. I deposited well over one thousand dollars, and my mom gave me a crash course on how to record deposits and withdrawals in the manual account register the credit union handed me.

My mom used this opportunity as a teaching moment to share her expectations and to help me devise a plan for how I would spend the money. My mom made the purpose clear. I was to save a portion for the unexpected, and spend the rest preparing for the necessities of college and dorm life. I personally want all kids to experience the pride and sense of responsibility I gained when my mom took me to open my first account.

Go One Step Further—Invest

Different fish require different bait, so when it comes to saving money, it will only create wealth for you if the money is invested wisely and in the right place. As your child sets their savings goals, it is appropriate to teach your children how to maximize their savings efforts. I encourage you to read and share the popular parable of the talents in Matthew 25:14–30 with your child. This parable is often used as an example of being a good steward and maximizing the financial resources we have been blessed to receive. In this parable, a rich man delegates the management of his wealth to his servants while he is away from home, much as investors in today's markets do. He gives five talents (a large unit of money) to the first servant, two talents to the second, and one talent to the third. Two of the servants earn 100 percent returns by trading with the funds, but the third servant hides the money in the ground and earns nothing. When the rich man returns, he rewards the two who made money, but severely punishes the servant who did nothing. Using this parable as a foundation, you can begin to introduce simple ways your children can invest their money.

A Lesson from My Dad

As a child, I loved getting the mail from the mailbox. We had a magazine subscription to *Ebony Jr!* where I found a pen pal in Boston that I would write regularly. Each week anticipating a letter from my pen pal, I'd see envelopes from the US Treasury Department addressed to my dad. Every few weeks, that same envelope with an orange insert and block letters would come in the mail. I later learned that my dad was purchasing US Savings Bonds with every paycheck. He'd place these envelopes on the top of his dresser drawer where they were earning interest for a greater return some time in the future. From the simple everyday task of collecting the family mail, my dad modeled the concept of saving and investing consistently.

Fast-forward fifteen to twenty years, and US Savings Bonds are moving toward extinction, but there are certainly other tools we can use to expose our children and teach them how investing works.

How Investing Works

Investing tools help our money grow faster through the power of compound interest. Compound interest is when you earn interest on both the money you've saved and the interest you earn.

This concept can be explained conceptually by using two real twenty-dollar bills and asking your child to place or hide them somewhere. Then ask the following questions:

- If we come back in six months or a year, will the money still be there?

- What could happen to it? Could you lose it, forget where you put it? Could it be stolen? Could you spend it?

- If it's still there, did it magically make more money?

You can then explain that if you put the bills in a bank, it will multiply. When you put your money in the right account and put it to work, it becomes your employee. It works so you don't have to.[8]

When it comes to selecting an investment option for your child, I recommend starting with

8   Denise Watson. "How to Teach Your Kids Compound Interest." http://www.thecreditsolutionprogram.com/how-to-teach-your-kids-compound-interest.

things they can touch, feel, or track online. Besides a savings account at your local bank or credit union, here are two additional examples:

- **Certificate of Deposit (CD).** CDs have the advantage of offering higher interest rates than savings accounts; however, individuals purchasing a CD must commit to holding it for a period of time, generally ranging from six months to five years or more. In exchange for locking your money away, CDs usually offer higher returns than a regular savings account, but they also have penalties if you withdraw before the maturity date. For the young investor, look for a no-penalty CD, with no minimum balance to introduce and help them learn how this tool works.

- **Dividend stock.** Dividend stocks are stocks of companies that give a portion of their quarterly profits back to shareholders. I first heard of this from my former boss who explained how he gifts stock of a Fortune 500 company every year for Christmas to his then four-year-old niece. In his example, the profits are reinvested to purchase additional stock and build an established investment portfolio for her once she's old enough to manage it. What a great idea, and so easy to do as parents.

Since investments are typically long-term tools, help your child develop their own reasons for saving. Here are some reasons to invest that you can discuss with your children:

- Education

- Personal interests/dreams

- Business

- Legacy

- Retirement

Overcome Saving Obstacles

Saving, like most healthy money habits, is a learned behavior. Similar to fishing, you have to be persistent and you have to be patient. Saving is a money discipline that requires practicing self-control and delayed gratification. To teach delayed gratification, let's look at the famous Stanford marshmallow experiment[9], performed by Walter Mischel and a team of researchers in the late 1960s and early 1970s.

In this experiment, four-year-old children were presented with a marshmallow and told they could eat it right away, or wait fifteen minutes and receive two marshmallows later. Some children couldn't control themselves and ate the marshmallow immediately, while others managed to wait the full fifteen minutes and received the reward of a second marshmallow.

The researchers added variations to this simple test of temptation and in some of their studies, more children were able to resist the marshmallow temptation. Walter Mischel concluded that "preschoolers tended to wait longer when they were given effective strategies."[10]

This finding is good news! It means that we can actually do something positive to teach our

---

9 For more on the study, read: http://pages.uoregon.edu/ harbaugh/Readings/UGBE/Mischel%201989%20Science,%20Delay%20of%20Gratification.pdf.

10 Sarah Rameriz. "5 Easy Ways to Teach Kids Self-Control and Delayed Gratification." http://afineparent.com/ emotional-intelligence/delayed-gratification.html

kids about delayed gratification. Here are three research-tested strategies that you can try with your kids and apply to saving money.

1. **Avoidance.** When the researchers covered the marshmallow, the children didn't need special strategies to avoid eating it. The children soon forgot about the marshmallow that was no longer visible or present. This same strategy can be used when it comes to saving money by immediately placing savings in a bank account or placing your child's savings money jar away once they place money in it.

2. **Distraction.** Similar to avoidance, distraction isn't necessarily the same as "out of sight, out of mind"; however, children waited longer for the second marshmallow when the researchers told them to "think fun thoughts." Distraction can be used when saving money as well. Instead of focusing on the how much (or little) money is in the savings jar, distract your child with challenges that will help them earn more money or spend less money to fuel their savings.

3. **Self-Directed Speech.** Although researchers didn't specifically instruct them in this strategy, some of the children chose to engage in self-directed speech in order to help themselves wait. They repeated phrases to themselves like, "I have to wait so I can get two marshmallows." Engaging in self-directed speech were linked with longer wait times.

Parents should therefore teach phrases that are easy to repeat and that remind children to control their impulses. For example, when it comes to saving money, you can teach your child money affirmations like "I am good at saving money" or "Each day it becomes easier to save money."

If a few researchers were able to teach some kids to apply these strategies in a single fifteen-minute session, surely you can succeed with your own children. The important part is to be consistent in applying them. Another psychologist[11] who studies self-control has compared it to

---

11 Roy F. Baumeister. "The Sugary Secret of Self-Control NYT." http://www.nytimes.com/2011/09/04/books/review/willpower-by-roy-f-baumeister-and-john-tierney-book-review.html?_r=.

a muscle, noting willpower can be strengthened with exercise. By helping our children apply their best self-control strategies to delay gratification in everyday situations, we help them to develop better self-control overall.

Benefits of Saving Early

Teaching your children to save builds character and lays the foundation of being financially responsible adults. The benefits of teaching your children to save early are found in the magic of compound interest. The earlier they begin to save, the more money they will have over time to use and spend responsibly.

Chances are, this healthy money habit will prevent your children from spending money when they shouldn't and stop them from having too many unnecessary financial obligations later in life.

The life skills we are teaching will impress upon them that saving is possible, even if it's just a little. They will be equipped with the knowledge, education, and experience on how to save and the benefits of saving. As they grow older, they will have a foundational level of financial intelligence that they can continue to build on. If we don't teach our children how to save, we shouldn't expect them to practice saving as an adult.

Our objective is to be proactive, avoid procrastination, and increase their financial intelligence one activity at a time.

Recommended Activities:

When it comes to learning concepts like saving and investing, visuals and physical interaction are important, especially for young children. With that in mind, here are a few ideas to teach your child how to save:

- **Save for a rainy day!** A portion of every home chore "commission," monetary gift, or cash reward received by your child should be placed in a savings jar, piggy bank, or a savings account. Similar to how my dad modeled savings for me through the purchase of a savings bond, we also want to encourage our children to save early in life.

- **Open a savings account.** There are many banks and credit unions that have savings accounts specifically designed for children. These programs may offer special rates and reward programs as the balances grow. You can physically visit a branch to open an account and have someone from the bank or credit union explain how it works. This can be the introduction to the banking system. Be careful to read all the fine print and find a participating financial institution that offers low- or no-minimum balance savings accounts. Saving money is tough enough, so make sure you gift your child a place to park their savings. I recommend opening a savings account at age thirteen.

🐟 **Celebrate and invest.** Purchase dividend stock for any celebration that typically includes gift-giving.[12] Birthdays, holidays, graduations. Make an investment in their future that allows them to see, touch and feel the quarterly dividends checks. I recommend sites like GiveAShare or UniqueStockGift for gift-giving.

---

12 For more on giving stocks for Christmas, read: http://time.com/money/3629345/everything-you-need-to-know-to-give-stocks-for-christmas/.

🐟 **Let's make a deal.** Once they are committed to saving for an item or experience, make an agreement that you will match the amount they save up to a certain amount. This exercise lends your support of their efforts, but also motivates them to save their money to reach the goal.

🐟 **Follow the market.** For children twelve and older, select one stock to follow based on your child's interest. For example, if their favorite athlete is sponsored by Nike, find the ticker symbol and follow the stock activity over the course of the year. Help them select two to three stocks based on their interests or favorite household products like Netflix or Coca-Cola. Look for resources that provide interactive simulations of the stock market like The Stock Market Game by Dianne Draze.

🐟 **Collective economics.** Introduce your child to the power of pooling one's resources together to achieve a common goal. You can begin the dialogue by explaining how you and your spouse pool your money together to provide for the family. Or how business partners bring different strengths and skills to form a successful business. This is a great activity if you have more than one child in your household. Allow them to dream up one thing they would like and would all benefit from. Maybe it's a gaming console, a video game, or a home computer. You can help them set a goal and allow them to work together to achieve it over time

🐟 **Encourage patience.** When your child sets a savings goal, use a calendar to mark off each day they save up for something. For example, tell your child to save for thirty days and mark each day that passes on the calendar. Consider adding incentives like matching their savings after they have saved for so many days. This exercise will encourage patience and delayed gratification on items they want to purchase.

Final Thoughts

Teaching your children how to save is an important step to prepare them for financial responsibility and a secure future. But it won't go very far if you don't practice what you preach and save for the future yourself. Whether we like it or not, most of us emulate the habits of our parents that we observed during childhood. In other words, you need to act how you want your children to act when they grow up.

In the next chapter, we will tackle the top hurdles in achieving financial success: mismanagement of credit and the overwhelming accumulation of consumer debt. Read on to see how you can influence your kids to make great choices and avoid the weight of living in debt.

Get the most out of this book by using the
supplemental workbook as you tackle
each money-management habit.

To reinforce the lessons you've learned in
Chapter 3: Save First and Consistently,
Refer to pages 17 – 20 in the workbook.

Download the printable workbook at
www.TheMasterPlaybook.com/free-workbook

CHAPTER 4

USE CREDIT RESPONSIBLY

"The rich rule over the poor,
and the borrower is slave to the lender."

—Proverbs 22:7(NIV)

In a society where credit and debt is so common, and where currently only five US states require high school students to take a class about money,[13] it remains our responsibility to warn our chil-

---

13 Jillian Berman. Only five states require high school

dren of the pitfalls and to teach them habits they can develop to use credit responsibly and to avoid the accumulation of consumer debt.

The objective of this chapter is to teach our children, primarily preteens and teenagers, the basics of how credit works, the concept of debt, the effective strategies to manage credit wisely, and how to avoid credit pitfalls in the future. While Proverbs 22:7 summarizes the relationship between the borrower and the lender, the Bible goes on in I Corinthians 7:23 (NIV) to encourage us not to be slaves to anyone. We have a responsibility to teach our kids to avoid the bait they will encounter.

Living in a Consumer Culture

We live in a consumer culture that accepts and promotes debt as a way of life. The Cambridge Advanced Learner's Dictionary describes our culture best: We are "a society in which people often buy new goods, especially goods that they do not need, and in which a high value is placed

---

students to take a class about money. http://www.marketwatch.com/story/teaching-about-money-does-your-state-make-the-grade-2015-10-20.

on owning many things." We are encouraged at every turn, whether through commercials, billboards, reality TV, or peer pressure, to buy the latest and greatest of everything. Our culture further promotes materialism and defines a person's self-worth and societal status based on worldly possessions.

Children represent an important demographic in this consumer culture, especially to marketers, because in addition to their own purchasing power, which is considerable, they influence their parents' buying decisions and are the adult consumers of the future.[14]

Marketers plant the seeds of brand recognition in very young children in the hopes that the seeds will grow into lifelong consumer relationships. According to the Center for a New American Dream, babies as young as six months of age can form mental images of corporate logos and mascots. Brand loyalties can be established as early as age two, and by the time children head off to school, most can recognize hundreds of brand logos.

---

14 Learn more here: http://mediasmarts.ca/marketing-consumerism/how-marketers-target-kids.

While fast food, toy, and clothing companies have been cultivating brand recognition in children for years, adult-oriented businesses such as banks and automakers are now getting in on the act.[15] Think of the music videos, sporting events, online games, and sponsored educational material or school events. Children are inundated with advertising.

Companies are creatively teaching our kids to indulge in the consumer culture. Consider Cool Shoppin Barbie[16] that came with her own credit card or online games that showed people using credit to pay for things.

Whether you know it or not, these tactics are teaching children about credit and perpetuate a culture of materialism and spending money they don't have. Because of kids' buying power and their influence with parents, marketers target teens as early as twelve years old to obtain credit cards. Teenage Research Unlimited shows 11 percent of teens ages

15 Ibid.

16 Vanessa Hua. "Parents Give Credit Card Barbie A Low Rating." http://articles.latimes.com/1998/apr/02/business/fi-35133.

twelve to nineteen have their own credit card; and another 10 percent have access to credit cards from their parents. Think about it: prepaid credit cards, VISA, MasterCard, and American Express gift cards are all credit cards with training wheels. They know that if young people obtain credit at a young age, they are more likely to keep the card and remain a customer for many years to come.

But don't get me wrong, these tools aren't all meant for evil. As parents, you can supplement these gift cards and prepaid debit cards by providing guidance on how credit works and teaching lessons on how to use credit responsibly—lessons my sisters and I stumbled through.

Explain to Your Child How Credit Works[17]

Depending on how early your children are introduced to credit cards and gift cards of their own, they may already have an idea of how credit works. Here's a brief overview of some key talking points you can use to explain how credit works.

---

17 Laura Adams. "How Do Credit Cards Really Work?" http://www.quickanddirtytips.com/money-finance/credit/how-do-credit-cards-really-work.

Credit cards are issued by a bank or other financial institution and are restricted to a maximum amount you can spend on the card. Gift cards are a form of credit where the maximum amount you can spend is placed on the card in advance.

The very act of using a credit card is borrowing money, which creates debt. When you borrow money from someone, you have to repay it. This is nonnegotiable and should be drilled into their understanding of credit cards. When you repay the money, you will have to pay back more than the amount that was given to you, and that additional amount is called interest. The interest paid is predetermined by the finance charge or annual percentage rate (APR) set by the bank, and each card company has different terms that vary. When finance charges (or interest) accumulate, that's when teens could end up with a massive bill that becomes difficult to pay off.

The good news is that you can teach your teenager to avoid all credit card finance charges by paying off the credit card balance before the due date. Making charges that can be paid off in full each month is the right way to use a credit card because you avoid paying interest. An even better strategy is for kids to save for the things they want and avoid using credit at all.

My First Credit Card

My freshman year in college, I was minding my own business passing through the Student Union when I was approached by an energetic twenty-year-old offering a cool t-shirt, water bottle, and key chain if I signed up for a credit card. Free stuff? Who doesn't like free stuff? Excellent! I signed up without hesitation and received the credit card in the mail within a few weeks. I didn't have a job and rationalized that having a credit card would be a great tool for emergencies. You know, just in case I ever needed it. Well, my emergencies turned into a shopping trip here and there, until I eventually racked up a few hundred dollars in credit card debt.

As I reflect on my personal introduction to credit and debt, I have a few quick takeaways:

1) I was lured in by cheap bait, and the consequences cost me hundreds of dollars.

2) At age nineteen, it was *waaaay* too easy to obtain credit. After all, I didn't have a job and the credit card company didn't seem to care.

3) I had never talked to anyone, including my parents, about credit cards or consumer debt,

so I started my journey by figuring it out through personal experience. Based on recent studies, I'm not the first. A recent survey shows high school students may receive some form of financial literacy training, where they cover topics like budgeting, but they don't cover debt or debt management.

4) While in college, I never used the credit card for a true need or emergency like books for a class or a flight home. Instead, I personally spent money I didn't have on non-essentials like trendy clothing and eating out at restaurants. While I racked up a few hundred dollars here and there, it would take almost another ten to fifteen years post-graduation for me to break the habit of spending money I didn't have.

Similar to my story, 55 percent of teenagers receive their first credit card during their freshman year in college.[18] There is a tendency for consumers, both

---

18 For further reading: http://www.cefe.illinois.edu/research/reports/credit%20card%20usage%20of%20college%20students_lsu_092003.pdf.

young and old, to take advantage of credit offers without thinking through the consequences of overspending. Overspending has enabled some 43 percent of Americans to spend more each month than they earn.[19] These poor spending habits and mismanagement of credit led me to include this topic in this book. Teenagers under eighteen are not able to obtain a credit card without an adult co-signing, so it is the parent's responsibility to monitor and manage their kid's first experience with credit cards. It is important to start talking to your children and teenagers about the concept of credit and debt before big business lenders reach them first.

More importantly, as parents you have to decide what your position is on your child using and having access to credit. It should be largely based on their maturity level and the amount of responsibility you believe they can handle. It can be very difficult for them to have access to a credit card and to pay if off consistently. The responsibility of managing a credit card requires discipline and

---

19 Learn more here: http://www.investopedia.com/articles/ pf/07/conspicuous_consumption.asp.

should be monitored by parents. Parents need to drill into the minds of their teenagers that credit is not free money, and has to be paid off on time.

Based on my experience with young people, it is incredibly easy to stumble into a debt trap. All it takes is a brief lapse in judgment. My recommendation would be to teach your children how to live without credit by saving for the things they want.

Good Debt vs. Bad Debt

While my personal approach is to avoid debt, there are times in life when debt is used as a tool to accomplish greater things. Here are two simplified ways you can help your teenagers identify good debt versus bad debt:

Good debt is when borrowing money is done to purchase an appreciating asset like a school loan, real estate loan, or any other appreciating asset. I would specifically highlight that a loan to fund college tuition or to acquire a new trade or skill only falls in the good debt category if the coursework is completed and allows you to earn more money than you would have without it.

Bad debt is when the borrowed money is used to purchase an asset that will lose value as soon as it is bought, like an auto loan, or using a store credit card to purchase shoes or clothes. The moment clothes or shoes are worn, the value of that item decreases.

Effective Strategies to Manage Credit Wisely and Minimize Debt

Through my personal experiences and coaching others to reduce their debt balances, I've learned and now preach that debt does not have to be a way of life. Operating in a digital age, the convenience of applying and getting approved for credit has the potential of placing our young people in position to take on more than they can handle.

Here are seven strategies parents can teach their teenagers today to encourage them to manage credit wisely and minimize debt.[20]

- **Strategy 1: Beware of Marketing Traps.** Raise their consciousness of the marketing tactics used to suck them into buying things they don't need. As discussed ear-

---

20 http://credit.about.com/od/avoidingdebt/tp/how-to-avoid-credit-card-debt.htm.

lier, marketers target teens through commercials, online ads, product placement, and celebrity endorsements to influence what our children purchase or persistently nag parents to purchase. Point these tactics out until they become obvious and can be avoided. Refer to the recommended activities on ways to raise their awareness and reduce their influence.

- **Strategy 2: Save Consistently and Establish an Emergency Fund.** Explain that acquiring debt is not the only way to obtain the things wanted in life. Using college as an example, besides planning ahead and consistently saving money now, teens should apply for grants and scholarships or consider working part-time to avoid or minimize school debt.

- **Strategy 3: Don't Use Credit to Purchase Basic Needs.** Credit cards should not be used to buy everyday items like food, clothing, or gas for their car. Having to use credit cards to cover these types of purchases is a sign that they may be spending their money unwisely.

- **Strategy 4: Charge Only What You Can Afford.** Avoid credit card debt by purchasing things you really can't afford. If you can't afford to pay cash, you can't afford to charge it. Based on how much your child earns in commissions each week, or how much they earn per hour at a part-time job, have them calculate how many hours they would have to work to purchase the item they are looking to buy.

- **Strategy 5: Practice Restraint and Self-Control.** Imagine trying to fill a hole while someone shoveled out more dirt than you put in. Your hole would never get filled, would it? It's the same with debt. Learn to deny yourself and avoid impulse purchases on material items, especially on a credit card.

- **Strategy 6: Pay Your Balances in Full.** Pay your balance in full each month. If you want to avoid credit card debt, pay off your credit card balance every month. That way, you'll never carry a balance. You never have to worry about whether you can meet the minimum payment because your credit card has already been paid in full.

- **Strategy 7: Limit Your Number of Credit Cards.** The more credit cards you have, the more you can charge. You may have great self-control, but it's better that you don't tempt yourself with thousands of dollars in available credit. Cut down on the number of credit cards in your wallet to avoid credit card debt.

As your child approaches adulthood, these strategies will encourage them to live within their means and give them a baseline of rules to follow to avoid future debt pitfalls. These strategies should also be coupled with the money habits discussed previously like living by a budget (Chapter 2) and saving for the things they want (Chapter 3).

Recommended Activities:

Here are a few recommended activities you can use to expose your child to marketing influences, how credit is used, and managing debt.

- **Brand recognition.** Show your children a number of popular brands and logos and ask them to identify them. Ask them how they know the brands. Have them point out product placement during movies or television shows once you've explained it. The objective is to make them conscious of the marketing tactics targeted to them to spend money. Play a game while watching TV and ask your child to count how many food or restaurant commercials come on during dinnertime. Explain how marketing is used to inform *and* to influence how money is spent.

Family IOU. Create an IOU in the family for a week. For the next seven days, take on each other's chores or loan one another money. After week one is over, have an open dialogue about how it felt to owe someone else. What if the person you owed was mean to you, would that make a difference? What if you were not able to repay, what should happen? Explain the consequences of what happens in the real world when a debt is not repaid such as the likelihood of your possessions being repossessed and a negative credit score, which will tell future lenders that you are not a good payer.

Share your balance sheet. If you can muster true transparency for the sake of teaching your children, allow your children to have a good look at the liabilities you currently hold. List them from one through ten and have your child label them as good or bad based on the information we've discussed earlier in the chapter. Have an open dialogue about the good and the bad. If you carry more consumer debt than you should, explain the steps you are taking to minimize it.

Already in Debt?

If you have a teenager who has already incurred more debt than they can handle, in lieu of bailing them out, use it as a teachable moment like my mom did in a testimony my sister shared:

I thought I had gotten myself in a bad situation with several credit cards. I asked Mom to co-sign a debt consolidation loan for me. She gently declined, explaining that the loan was a "quick way out." Instead, she helped me figure out a plan to repay my creditors. I learned to manage my debt on my own without having to take on more debt. It was a valuable money lesson, and I was glad I could go to my mom for help.

Just as my mom came through for my sister in her early twenties, come to your child's rescue with these strategies:

- Create a debt reduction plan with your teen or young adult. I would recommend starting with the debt snowball method.[21]

- Lower the current credit limit on the card or take away the privilege altogether.

- Use a prepaid card that can be monitored by you.

Finally, review the strategies noted above to prevent them from incurring more debt.

Final Thoughts

You just learned the importance of talking to your kids about credit and debt now versus later. They are being heavily targeted and are already practicing using credit in the form of gift cards and even through mobile apps. Your guidance gives them

---

21 The Debt Snowball Method: https://en.wikipedia.org/wiki/Debt-snowball_method.

the knowledge they need to make wise decisions now before they have to make decisions that involve even larger sums of money when it comes to purchasing real estate or a car.

In the next chapter, you will gain insight on how to encourage a giving spirit with your child. Read on to gift this life lesson to your son or daughter.

Get the most out of this book by using the
supplemental workbook as you tackle
each money-management habit.

To reinforce the lessons you've learned in
Chapter 4: Use Credit Responsibly,
Refer to pages 21 – 24 in the workbook.

Download the printable workbook at
www.TheMasterPlaybook.com/free-workbook

CHAPTER 5

GIVE GENEROUSLY

"How can we expect our children to know and experience the joy of giving, unless we teach them that the greater pleasure in life lies in the art of giving rather than receiving?"

—J. C. Penney

One of the most important lessons from a parent is to teach your child how to be charitable. Teaching your child to give and to help others is one of the most productive methods to counter the consumer culture that encourages a "give me" impulse. This chapter will focus on giving, the life skill that will shape your children into good citizens, help them to be thankful for the things they have, and help them develop compassion and understanding for others. As such, it is an important habit for kids to be exposed to at an early age.

My childhood was filled with active service. There was always something to do and someone in need. I can vividly recall helping my mother feed needy families in our neighborhood who may have fallen on rough times due to job loss or long-term illness.

My mom volunteered weekly to manage the food bank at our church. We would shop for, stock, and organize the food bank shelves and freezer with canned goods, perishable items, and frozen meats from the Atlanta Community Food Bank. We prepared four or five boxes at a time, paying careful attention to load each box generously and equitably with an item from each major food group and considering each meal that would be made from the food items available.

I can remember feeling like I was running my very own store, and I especially loved being my mom's little helper. Those in need of food would make it known to the church office, and we'd load the car to personally deliver our creations. I witnessed the smiles and hugs people gave my mom as they retrieved the goodies from our car. Needs were met, people were grateful, and all was well in the world.

Actively participating and volunteering with my mom along with witnessing people's appreciation and gratitude were valuable experiences for me as a child. I learned empathy, kindness, and the importance of people taking care of each other. I also learned that helping others is a healthy habit where money can help fill a need, but that the value of sharing our time and our talent are equal, if not greater, contributions.

The Three T's of Giving

Giving is all about helping others. You can give to fill a need, to express love or encouragement, or to bring joy and happiness to the lives of other people. Teach your children the Three T's of Giving by using their Treasure, Time, and Talent. No matter the method, the goal is to make giving a routine within their daily lives.

The Gift of Treasures:

Giving of your treasures includes contributing money or other possessions to help others. Examples would be donating money so less-fortunate families can buy school supplies, or buying a toy for a child who may not otherwise receive a gift for their birthday or other special occasion. If someone in your family is suffering from an illness, consider saving money to give so researchers can find a cure. During Christmas, the whole family could donate money to a charity that has a special meaning.

The Gift of Time:

Giving time is another way children can give to other people. As parents, you have almost total control in how your child spends their time outside of school. Getting your children involved in service organizations is just as important to their development as having them play on a sports team or participate in a dance recital. Encourage your children to use their time doing something for others.

As a child, it may be one of the easier gifts to use. Children can give time to help a neighbor, the community, and the church. Ways to give that involve your child's time could include doing yard work for an elderly neighbor, distributing gloves and socks to the people in a homeless shelter, or picking up trash in the community.

The Gift of Talent:

We all have a special gift or skill to give and share with other people. Does your child like to sing or draw? Perhaps they have a special gift with using technology or putting things together. The very talents they could get paid for are the talents and skills they should offer at will to help someone in need or to actively contribute to a cause greater than themselves.

Lead by Example

One of the best ways to model this healthy habit is by example. A poll conducted by TheMint.org found that 77 percent of children under the age of seventeen are either not aware of their parents giving, or know that they give but do not how or to whom.[22]

---

22 http://www.talkaboutgiving.org/wp-content/up-loads/2011/04/TAG_whitepaper2.pdf.

When you are writing out a check for a charity or to an organization you believe in, it is important to include the kids in the conversation.[23] Let them hear and see that you set aside money for donations, and more importantly, explain why doing so is important to you.

When discussing what they should do with the money they earn, talk about how you decide how much to set aside for donating with your money. Remind your child from time to time how fortunate they are—not just to have food and shelter, but to also have a family that loves them.

The same principle goes for volunteering your time and talents. Where appropriate, include your children in your volunteer activities and service projects and talk about what volunteering your time and talents mean to you. I'm not suggesting you drag them to every event, but you also shouldn't hide your everyday acts of kindness. If you're taking dinner to a friend who has just been released from the hospital, say so. If you help raise funds for worthy causes through

---

23 http://kidmoney.about.com/od/Values/fl/How-to-Teach-Your-Child-About-Charitable-Giving.htm.

your church, temple, or local community group, talk about it.

By talking about where and how you give, you not only show your kids the importance of giving, but you're sharing your values about the issues that matter most to your family—whether you're passionate about supporting the arts, cleaning up the environment, assisting the elderly, or raising money to find a cure for cancer.

When they see and hear about how you practice the three T's, they will be more inclined to do so as well.

Benefits and Why Giving Is Important

"Life's most persistent and urgent question is, 'What are you doing for others?'"

—Martin Luther King, Jr.

Helping others can teach children invaluable life lessons. Giving can balance out a child's natural selfishness and persistent desires for toys, games, and other things our consumer culture convinces them to want. Instead, giving to those in need can help increase your child's appreciation of the things she has in her own life.[24]

Another great benefit of teaching a child how to be charitable is that donating their treasure, time, and talent gives children a powerful boost in self-esteem. In time, your child will realize their acts of kindness can make a difference in someone's life. The idea isn't just to inform or expose your child to some of the pain and suffering in the world, but to give your children the great gift of thinking and knowing that they have the power to help make the world a better place.

By incorporating giving into your everyday lives, you will bring out the natural helper in your child, preteen, or teenager. As children grow, so do their opportunities for making a difference. Before you know it, your child may be taking the lead in choosing charitable projects for your family or identify a need they would like to take on themselves.

Teach your children these three key principles of giving:

---

24 http://childparenting.about.com/od/familyhome/a/Volunteer-Ideas-For-Kids.htm.

- **Give with purpose.** Being able to give to others is a blessing and should be done on purpose. What I mean is, giving to others is so important that you should *plan* to give to others. Include giving in your spending plan. Similar to saving, giving should be a mandatory line item in every budget. After you have saved and covered the costs of your basic needs (I purposely did not mention wants), you should plan to give. Oftentimes, we are able to sacrifice our wants in order to give and really bless someone in need. "He answers and said to them, He that has two coats, let him impart to him that has none; and he that has meat, let him do likewise" (Luke 3:11, AKJV).

- **Give from the heart and with pure intentions.** The size of the gift is not important; however, the intention behind giving is very important. While it is important to acknowledge and encourage our children to be selfless, please try to avoid going overboard with praising your child. The objective is to make sure that children avoid giving for reward, recognition, or expecting something in return. The Bible warns of this in Matthew

6:1 (AKJV): "Take heed that you do not your alms before men, to be seen of them: otherwise you have no reward of your Father which is in heaven."

- **Connect your giving with your talent or interests.** Make it easy for children to give by connecting with an organization or charity that matches their interests and talents. For example, if your child is active, consider signing up for a walk-a-thon or bike-a-thon where they can raise money by doing things they enjoy. Be sure to get your child's input on what charities the family can support.

When your child feels a part of the decision-making, they are more likely to become interested in the process.[25] Offer your child a few choices of things they might want to do or people they might like to help. Would your daughter like to read books to children in a hospital? Would your son prefer helping you plant trees in the community park? If your child wants to help animals, search online

25 http://childparenting.about.com/od/socialdevelopment/a/charitablechild.htm.

for agencies or foundations that place animals in healthy environments.

Recommended Activities:

Here are a few recommended activities you can complete as a family, but more importantly to demonstrate ways your child can practice being charitable.

- **Teach your child to tithe.** If you attend church, your child can begin donating there. While the Old Testament offers 10 percent as a guideline for tithing, the important first step is simply to give something, no matter the amount. The tithe helps your local church and/or ministries so they can help do more for the Kingdom of God. As they learn more about giving, they can begin to give in proportion to God's blessings (Luke 12:48).

- **Charity box.** Mark a container in your home that can be routinely filled with gently used clothing and toys to donate to those less fortunate. The clothes and toys can be things that the family has outgrown or are no longer used or needed. Make a trip to a charity that needs it and personally deliver the items.[26]

🐟 **Care packages for the homeless.** Assemble care packages that can be personally delivered to a homeless shelter or kept in the car and shared in a spontaneous opportunity. The contents of the care packages could include bottled water, peanut butter crackers, socks, and a tissue pack. Download the supplemental workbook for more examples of items you can place in each care package.

🐟 **Donate hair to cancer patients.** Has your teen reached a stage where he or she wants to cut their long locks of hair? Encourage them to donate what many would love to have and serve chemotherapy patients, or children their age plagued with illnesses that prevent their hair from growing.

🐟 **Cards and appreciation packages to those in the military.** Do you know someone serving in the military? Consider sending them a

26 For more inspiration, read: http://kidmoney.about. com/od/charity/tp/teach-kids-charity.htm.

handwritten thank-you note or holiday card to let them know they are appreciated. You could also prepare an appreciation package that includes candy, gum, reading material, crossword puzzles, a t-shirt for their home baseball team, playing cards, and any number of things that you think the person would appreciate, especially if they are serving overseas.

Select a charity based on your child's interests. As I mentioned earlier, the best way to involve your child is to allow them to serve and help others based on their personal interests. When looking for a charity to donate money to, have your child go to a site such as Charity Navigator, an online resource used to make sure the charity is using the money for the actual cause. You are looking for charities that give a large portion of their funds to the actual programs they run and not to administrative expenses, such as payroll and fundraising.

Final Thoughts

As we wrap up our final chapter and lesson on giving, I am immediately reminded of how Jesus fed more than 5,000 people from five loaves of bread and two fish—all because of a young boy's generosity. The story is found in John 6:5–13 (NLT) and certainly one I encourage you to share with your child to illustrate the difference one person can make. In addition to making a difference, establishing a healthy giving habit with children is a surefire way for them to learn to be appreciative for the things they have and to have empathy for those who do not have.[27]

In learning the art of fishing, you have to be willing to get your clothes wet and your hands dirty. Similarly, in wanting a better financial future for your child, you have to equip them with the tools and the strategies every child needs to master their money. Each of the five money-management habits covered in this book will establish the financial foundation your child will need and use as they maneuver through life.

Revisit these chapters as your child matures and grows, download the workbook, and continue to share, teach, and explore with your child. As

---

27 http://lauragraceweldon.com/2013/06/27/40-ways-kids-can-volunteer-toddler-to-teen/.

these money-management habits are taught and practiced, the principles and concepts will produce positive, long-lasting results.

Get the most out of this book by using the
supplemental workbook as you tackle
each money-management habit.

To reinforce the lessons you've learned in
Chapter 5: Give Generously,
Refer to pages 25 – 29 in the workbook.

Download the printable workbook at
www.TheMasterPlaybook.com/free-workbook

ACKNOWLEDGMENTS

To my sisters, Leslie, Toni, and Bridget: your love, support, and prayers have carried me thus far. Without all of you, I would not be the person I am, and I thank you for believing in me.

To Bishop Dale C. Bronner: thank you for allowing God to use you. Your inspiring messages week after week fed my soul, pushed me to pursue my passion, and reassured me I was meant to run this race.

To Ebony Stubbs, Kimberly Mays, Basheerah Enahora, Erika Lewis, and Jeannine Brown: our accountability calls and dream-casting sessions, coupled with your creativity and practical advice, have helped me turn this dream into a reality, and for that, I am grateful.

Last, to Chandler Bolt, Remy Vance, Pam Burke, the SPS Mastermind Community, and my incredible launch team: thank you for your positive energy, suggestions, and generosity. Your enthusiasm propelled me to achieve this milestone!

ABOUT THE AUTHOR

As a personal finance advocate, Holly Reid is on a mission to motivate, inspire, and help others manage their finances as responsible stewards. Holly's philosophy is grounded in the basic principles of living debt-free, saving for the future, and investing wisely. She believes each person has the power to create a healthy financial future.

She is a Certified Public Accountant and finance professional with over 15 years of experience serving the media and entertainment industry. She currently offers her expertise through interactive sessions designed to educate and inform groups on how to apply financial principles and promote financial literacy to teenagers and young adults. Her knack for connecting with people, coupled with her sincere interest in helping others experience financial peace, make her an ideal mentor to coach individuals to achieve their personal financial goals.

As the youngest of four siblings, Holly is no stranger of doing more with less. Exposure to the broad economic landscape, and its disparities, piqued her interest to understand money management and propelled her to discover savvy ways to save and experience financial harmony as an adult. Furthermore, her personal financial mistakes and re-bounds now fuel her to build a legacy worth leaving.

CONNECT WITH THE AUTHOR

www.TheMasterPlaybook.com

If you enjoyed this book, please leave a review on Amazon and Goodreads, and connect with The Master Playbook on social media.

 TheMasterPlaybook

 @TheMasterPlaybook

 @MasterPlaybook

Made in the USA
Columbia, SC
18 December 2019

85270224R00067